Decency

Decency

poems

Marcela Sulak

Black
Lawrence
Press

Black
Lawrence
Press

www.blacklawrence.com

Executive Editor: Diane Goettel
Book and cover design: Amy Freels

Published 2015 by Black Lawrence Press.
Printed in the United States.

Contents

Dear Fernando Cortés

Ecclesiastes

Katamon, Jerusalem

It's so nice to be pretty and wearing polka dots
on a swinging dress with a small cinched waist
pushing a blue-eyed child through
the trade winds in her pram. The trees
are swaying, and on the bench below them
an old woman looks up through the boughs
to a parcel of clouds; when she sees us she smiles.
When we pass she stands up and begins with her
zlata moje, my golden child, and she reaches to
touch our cheeks, and her hand stays outstretched,
and she's asking for just a little of our gold, something
for the bus or for lunch or, I reach into my tiny purse,
drop some coins, since her hand is now the meter
that turns us in our slot.

Chocolate

The day I won the custody case my lawyer gave me a bitter chocolate
in black and silver paper. Once I saw cacao pods
drying in a Venezuelan village square

during Easter week; through the open church doors, peeling saints sniffed
    and were carried
like colicky children through night streets. The local hot chocolate
was thickened with cornmeal and canella bark

somebody tore from the trees. To reach that village we found a fisherman,
    plowed
through rows of porpoises, then hiked five kilometers
inland through banana and cocoa trees,

which like shade. Once only men could drink
chocolate. Women were permitted cacao beans as currency,
to buy meat or slaves or pay tribute. It feels good to imagine a single seed,

hidden in the forbidden mouth, the tongue
curled, gathering the strength to push. The Aztec king discarded
each gold-hammered cup after its initial use; his chocolate was red as fresh
    blood.

He was a god to them. It was frothy,
poured from great heights. When we bathed in the village river, girls
gathered around me, whispering, why is your skin so pale? Why is your
    hair so straight?

Can we braid it? *Dime, eres blanca?*
The judge, our lawyers, her father, and I decided the fate
of my child. The dark liquid we poured was ink, initialing our little
    negotiations.

Who can know the heart of another, the blood
spiced with memory, poured from one generation to the next
over great distances? The Mayan word for chocolate means *bitter*. The
    village

used to be a plantation; now it is a co-operative, owned by descendants
of the former slaves. At Easter Vigil the women lined up
behind the most beautiful, in a long sky

-blue dress adorned with gold stars. Between the decades of the rosary she
    called out,
while we shuffled our feet in merengue beat, bearing the saints
through the streets, someone shot off a Roman

candle. The men's procession paused for rum. I know I'll be paying for it
    the rest
of my life. The Mayan word means *bitter water*. The cacao
tree was uprooted from paradise.

La Malinche's Love Letters to Fernando Cortés

1. No body of water is named for Cortés.

I rarely think of him embodied
when I think of him.

The natives are always
the inverse:
white-as-blank-page moths,
drawn by
the dark light of reason.

These mornings I awake—pushing
back the covers
of a slowly closing tome—into
that dark spot
-lit void we all assume
is the stage.

Between the sturdy banks of his voice,
I like how my tongue flows.

2. As his translator,

there was nothing I feared
more than his silence,
except the words against
which the world receives
her degradations.

He said the streets were paved in gold.
He said the streets were paved.
He said there were streets.
He said there, there.

3. Cartography

If there is one
true road only,
as the friars say,
there must be
many maps, and their
cacophonous cartographers, drawing
our attention to the
similarity between it
and a golden tongue

They call me *La Chingada*,
because of him,
but it was my mother
who sold me,
and didn't I make a
map so fine
you could fill every loss
with a world?

4. Vacation photos from the new Eden

Usually
I travel local transportation
systems,
snapping photos from dusty
windows.

Dead-
pan, our secular approximations
trip
across the photographic paper
of the divine.

5. Mother & father gods

Wild teosinte is very small and hard to open.
It seemed impossible in the beginning, seven,
eight, twelve thousand years ago, that anything
would come of it. But then an ear of corn appeared,

and from it, the mother and father gods.
We are beyond all that now. We haven't yet
learned to inhabit that world. And yet
its wet footprints reappear in dreams of drought.

The seven famished cows consume
the seven succulent ears. We have about
the same chance at surviving in the cupule
of an "us," wrapped in green shucks,

as the future has at miscarriage—though
she is growing older every year, and so
one can always *wait without hope, for hope
would be hope for the wrong thing.*

6. Circumstances under which you may resign

The anorexic stomach
clenches
its swallowed fist
of food.
It's wrong, Cortés,
to say,

to consume beauty, you must
completely break
with it. It must come to you
on a platter
from outside. You must arrange
yourself, too,
so that your inner ugliness

does not disrupt your pleasure.
Anything I say,
you say, will be caressed
until it comes
to resemble a truth we once
read about.

If only he would have
liked me a little, it would
have made such a difference.
It would have changed everything.

7. Gold

Here they are, those cornfields
that led Cortés to claim
the streets of Tenochtitlan
were paved in gold. Whose
ankles swished through them today
to meet a minor destiny?
I carried our son through
those very fields the day
he was born, *mestizo*,
mestizo, translated across
Cortés's pollinating tongue.

8. Cortés's vanity

One evening you described the void
between the pillars of your world,
which you have dressed in the most modest clothes

and never mention in public. How your face,
reclining on the unflattering yellow sofa, finally
looked its age. It was a relief.

How I would have loved
to stand one night with you
under a meteor shower

and let some other entity
cascade its celestial seed all over the world. And could
you hold my hand and squeeze until I returned

from the skies I rarely visit anymore
to the yellow sofa, now
smelling faintly of drought.

9. You can call me mother, of course

They call me *La Malinche*,
because I betrayed. Cortés called me
Doña Marina. Our friends

called us by the same name.
You can call me mother,
of course. But what I like most,

is the unanswered calling in the sun
and the corn and the coins, those luminous
voices eternally seeking their gods.

Translation depends, not on what must be included, but on what must not be left out.

after Idra Novey

You enter the country next door from under the stone
Church of the Redeemer

subway exit. *No Pork Chinese Restaurant*
and *Mr. Chicken*, flank the avenue

both sides *strictly halal*.
The immigrant stories conclude happily

thus far: love at first sight ends
in marriage. The NGO administrator

can finally quit the dead-
end job and be a stay-at-home mom, lobbying

to remove the ice-cream truck from the park.

The baby sons resemble their mothers
or else their paternal grandfathers. Slender men in bright shirts

lean against shiny, long black sedans, smoking
cigarettes. It is both the spawning grounds

and the death place of fiction.
The little ones learn to become miniature

predators themselves, until they encounter others
of their own kind. An aggregation

is called a school.
Visitors must check their own children

at baggage claim;
are either conveniently

or conspicuously
bilingual,

depending on their income level.
The average rainfall is silver

and distributed equally throughout the seasons.
What the bible really says instructors stand

in neat skirts beside their docile placards,
waiting for you to ask them to dance.

There is no binary opposition—identity is where and what time
you stand to put your make-up on,

relative to the points of time in space
of those around you,

their handfuls of brightly colored plastic,
their recession so slow you don't

notice it at first. Polyphony is certainly possible, too,
indeed, it is the preferred

method of communication, for the birds
are sky-bound at present.

The inhabitants are friendly and curious, and the military
carry their cameras carelessly,

with the safeties off and the barrels
aimed haphazardly at everything.

Men on Strike

Men on parade. Men
migrant Hispanic and red
necks in long hair clean

shaven the kind my
daddy bought parts from never
touching some of them

could rewire your grand
ma's house sharing their wife's tort
illas. They'd have stopped on

the narrow shoulder
of the highway to help you change
a flat or driven to town

to fill up the gas
can they were lending you or
given you a jump in

the near-deserted
parking lot, and here they are
now—embarrassed as

hell, like you had asked
them to hug their neighbor's wife
in church at the kiss

of peace, you know they
secretly like it. The men
I like most answer

not yet instead of
none that I know of some wear
Cuban heels and tight

jeans and spin when they
dance you. The tall black Southern
leader counter clock

wise keeps time today
calling *whoooo's the man*? Calling
who'sgonnago? In

sharp beats—merengue
they are embarrassed to dance
with invisible

partners called *below*
minimum wage! Insufficient
benefits! Every

one looking attract
ing attention the fact of
bodies as things with

needs where before there
had been only necklace links
impossibly de

licate their daughters
brought them unknotting themselves
beneath thick fingers

engines shuddering
to the quick strike of a spark
plug the free combusting

that which a casing
contains all the invisible
forces that keep the machines

of the world worlding
and pinned to the self-cleaning
sky. Chrysler building

in full bloom, forgive them they
feel bad, like they ruined a play
ground. This one here, where

just past Broadway the Grace
building slides to a stop at
their feet.

Decency

At the end of our marriage, I remember
the raccoons of my childhood that came to steal our corn,
the king-snake asleep in a barrel of feed, nipped by my coffee-can scoop
then his smooth brass coils around my wrist, and how in panic
I took a BB gun and shot him, and how my father
whipped me good for killing a decent, harmless creature.
And how my brother set the spring-triggered steel jaw trap for the coons
in the dim light of the barn floor; my cat stepped into it and caught her paw,
and how she howled, her desperate twist, and when I bent to release her
she bit my finger and it swelled ten times its normal size, how that's what
    happens,
my father said, when you touch an animal in pain.

Louise, TX

Where I am, it is Texas now,
a constellation

of suns caught in the lemon
tree. No one calls

the monarch butterfly *gringo*,
dusty sage, eternal

bleed of the salvia as if
something the wind scratched. Time

a communal thing
-amajig. Property. This morning

I stepped on a translucent baby
gecko I injured

fatally. My mother said maybe
it will recover,

set it outside. She
has changed. Forgive me.

In the tender
rain-filled grass, bouquet of Angus

calves fluttering their lashes,
they watch my mother

and me pass. Tomorrow
they'll be meat. But today their ears

twitch in the surprise
of a south-eastern breeze

that, for all
they know, will never end.

A Body in Labor

is a verb composed entirely of tenses
tensions and tents
      recast as curtains
            in the windows of the accidental railroad town
attenuations:
      the freighted car quivering down the tracks taking the future
      with her.

It's not really a language
it's a way of live.
      Foreman's burly grimaces = *ponga el hierro aquí.*
      Foreman's burly grin = *éso, cabrón!*

Foreman's foreplay: drafted maps
      provisional timetables, coffee stained and folded
            on the nightstand by the metal bed.

A body in labor
is a verb composed entirely of contracts.
      Your grandmother giggling:
            Some of us got caught.

A body in labor is a translator
busy loading scrap metal into waiting cars
28 lbs at a time
            assembly line dancing
            whistling lunch pail
            your immigrant grandfather.

Now you are being directed to a site of authentication.
        I is no I there.

Translation demands consistency.
Whatever you say on a satellite phone
will be mimed by the planets in slow motion
afterwards for years.
Repetition and recollection:
the same movement   but in opposite directions.

Baron Hungerford (who wasn't really a baron)
named the three insouciant towns Edna, Louise, and Inez
for his three daughters at home in France.
They never grew up.

Translation Theory:
one body in labor is equal
to all other bodies in labor   separate but equal
provided each body is laboring equally   is producing equal
numbers of products
in any given interval.

Fatigue is a collapsing box
of temporary placeholders.
        I is no I there.

Pain derives its meaning from reference points:
        the seconds between contractions
        the dry spots between water drops
        little squeezes in between memoranda
but as general, one doesn't remember
much.

Post is a great example of a reference point.
Love does not alter when it alteration finds.

The History of the Papaya

The papayas nudge
each other when attached, their
trunk shifts. They are blind

sleepy, wrapped in leafy
shadows, piled into trucks
before the morning

breaks. Nevertheless
our mother is beginning
to doubt the veracity

of our adopted
brother's claim he watched his friend
starve at four in a crack

house in America,
their biological moms
felled across mattresses.

Another brother
listens to Rush Limbaugh loud,
his tool box opened

on the disc harrow.
I expected more of this
cracked farm dirt over

which red-tailed
hawks and gas fumes lift—any
arc a promise. When

cutting papaya
you can see in the slits of
their yellow sides a

hundred open eyes,
which ones, you think, favor you.

Solidarity

for I. V. V.

i. Araceli

Contigo, se puede compartir el silencio, me dijo.
Por eso te amo.

And it's true, silence is the sheet over my bare body
when I am being examined by her words, when I am stretching

my fingertips into the glove of her words, when I am filing
their fingernails, when I am trimming their split ends,

when I am threading her words with flowers,
notes or rain,

when I am kneading the neck muscles of her words, for
they are stiff with *all those men staring*

at your hair, staring at your body, her husband said.
So she shaved her head.

Afterwards her words begin to gain weight
and luster.

ii. Yael

I know how women usually talk. It's how I talk: "sorry
for the strange diction of this email, I've been writing

a sonnet and am stuck in the 15th century," and you say, "wow,
you are capable of writing a sonnet

at 9 pm? By 8:30 I'm in bed." And I say, "it's not a very good
sonnet. And also by the time I get myself out of bed

you've already done more than I'll do all day." And you say, "but
my house," and I say,
                              this is a poem about the silence
we unraveled ourselves in,

not the one with the gag in the mouth, the hand over
the ransom money it took her family 2 weeks to come up with.

iii. Araceli

Who will take care of your sister when I die? her mother asked her,
rhetorically. Once when she was twelve she accompanied her father,

because her mother was taking care of the blind sister,
to the capitol. When she reached

her fingers into a conch shell filled with white powder she assumed
was sugar her father shook his head

very slightly. Two months after the kidnapping he flew her
to Miami. In her country it was still illegal.

The return trip landed in a new city where the family had gathered in
a new house and the father settled into his new job.

No one knew them here.
It's one of the last things she told me

about herself. Usually we spoke about Sor Juana
or made mole. Everything I know about tequila is hers.

Usually we screamed with laughter.
It's her story, her silence. She shared it with me. Am I so great

because she shared it?
Because it was secret? What now that I am sharing it?

iv. Texas

Because silence is sliding, hands behind his back, over the cracked-mud pond
in a field where people like you were massacred

and where mosquitoes bred, and before they were slaughtered they smeared
alligator grease on their skin to keep their blood

from being spilled by the mosquitoes. That's what Texas is,
and the murdered Karankawa also massacred others—

v. about Martin

—he played bass guitar in church choir at the 6 pm Sunday mass
was an only child of a single mother.

went to nursing school and lived with a charming man named Doug,
a paraplegic, to pay for university. He was an Italian literature major

who could not go to Italy because he had no visa to come back home with,
had no passport, no citizenship. Martin wasn't born here you know

when he was 8. With his mother, across the Chihuahua Desert—you know,
with a coyote and backpack   uncle in Texas

let's call this silence a pocket in which you plunge your fist. In which you
stuff the lizards you found in the desert, in which you hide your surprises.

I think, he said, *I am my mother's rape.*
This scarf I am wearing now   from Chiapas, first place Martin visited
          when he

got his citizenship. It is black and warm for the desert, woven by people
who feed him well call him cousin nephew grandson, happy.

They ate silence, the stew of generations.
                              And to embody your words.

vi. Virginity

It's not that you get tired, it's that it starts to be the only thing,
starts to disappear you.

Your parents phone you at college to ask: how is your virginity
doing? Did your virginity have a good day?

What does it want to be when it grows up? Your virginity sounds
a little sad this morning. What kind of cake does your virginity want

for its birthday? your girlfriends saw the most amazing shoes
that your virginity would look terrific in!

Want to go shopping? your boyfriends—would your virginity like to see
a movie? What about dinner?

vii.

Let's call this silence the file hidden in the cake
the water bottles strategically placed in the Arizona desert border.

viii. Sister

       the hug between my sister and me when we looked down at our feet
          and saw we were wearing the same exact pair of boots though

                we'd not spoken in two years.

And I knew it was   I mean,   we probably all knew it was
But she was also a strong character. and he never physically hit her.

and I did tell her I thought she should leave him
whenever she brought it up,   but I also added

just remember who his parents are.   And remember
where you live. And what it will be like to be a divorced

mother of two
in that place, and decide

what is easier to live with. you know he'll let you have the children
without a fight,

the eggshells we walked on, no that we slid our bodies over
when we were snakes, our

tongues flickering out to test the heat of the moment with words,
our tongues dipping in the broken shells for a little taste of yolk,

a drop of the little sun
we broke,

the silence on our tongues cushioning a *hello*—and then
the next words—*I forgot*—and then the next words,

would you mind
and when that went without incident, *would you mind*

turning the car around, I forgot—the explosion igniting the entire block
we had to retrace...

ix. witches

My daughter is named for my grandmother, a midwife
who attended the births of 90 babies in rural Texas

before they had cars and after they finished having witches
but before there were doctors. Now you may understand

what I mean when I say another woman
gave my daughter a book called "The witches and the rabbi"

for her birthday. Here is the plot: a village is terrorized by a plague
of witches who fly from their cave when the moon is full,

on brooms through the sky except when it's raining. I'm not sure
what the witches actually do to the village, since no one

actually goes outside on those nights. Gary, Indiana, could use
an infestation of witches—no stabbings

or gunshot wounds on evenings of full moons.
But one full moon when it is raining the rabbi shows up

with twenty townsmen. The witches
are so delighted they make them a feast of all the good things

they have. The rabbi tricks them into dancing with him and
the vigilante men, out into the rain,

which kills them. I knew her father's mother was secretly
glad when I started to hemorrhage. She didn't want me

to have a homebirth with a midwife.
"What kind of rabbis are these?"

Says my rabbi, stopped by for a quick hello. My daughter
wanted to show him that we had a book about rabbis. "They're

engaging the poor witches
in mixed dancing and leading them astray," he says.

This is the broom which sweeps the sky of the stars you have
to be too drunk to write about, as Daisy put it.

This is the housework the princesses do disguised
as village maidens. These are the constellations that form

in the shadow of the stars.
Silent are the women in the village

who took their cloth packets of herbs and were silent
when their husbands rushed off to kill the witches in that story.

x. Chorus with sister

The head of PR in Curacao's biggest bank once told me *you can be*
a banker or an accountant or a professor or a writer, but at home

you are always a woman.
        We were having a drink involving Curacao blue in a local bar;

it was ghastly, but the floating market was better, the funchi divine.
You are always a woman at home, dushi.
                                        , raped and cut up 21 year old

, his mother had the courage to walk across the desert
with him as a young child so he could have a life and study Italian

literature and nursing.

And to embody your words.
                        being good southern girls my sister and I imagined

and I curled her hair for the wedding—my sister couldn't bear
our mother with us in the bathroom,

we'd thought the beige carpet, the peach colored wallpaper
was so beautiful when it was

        new. I applied her eyeshadow. I don't remember
what we'd talked about. Only that I'd insulted her future

father-in-law
        the night before, at the rehearsal dinner,

but she didn't bring it up. Probably we just talked about the make-
up and the hair. And at

the ceremony a few hours later the priest kept calling her
my name, so maybe it meant they weren't actually married

after all.

xi. The speaker

and it's good to say I don't even think about it any more—sometimes I
think
I made it up, my mother asking me what I was wearing after I told her

—and it was mostly true. I don't think about it anymore—
but sometimes I still wake up from a dream that my face

has been slashed till it looks like
a net has been cast over it.

and then I go back to sleep so that in the next dream Sabrina
can lay her hands over my

face and the cuts close and my skin heals.
Did you know the word for cosmic and cosmetic are the same root?

Silence, be the bathmat I step on from a steaming bath, be the towel,
the soap, be the sleep, the toast on which the jam of the day is spread

the godly fabric, the network of roots that hold the topsoil of earth
in place, the warp of time, the bubble of it, the love so vast

there are no longer lovers to rise from its clay, no god to blow
breath into them, the injury and injured and the

injuring, the hate and the healing and the force that holds
them together, closer than breath, *contigo*

se puede compartir el silencio.
Wherever you are right now, *companera de silencio,* I am with you,

on your tongue, curling it into the laugh, into the quietest
shout in the world.

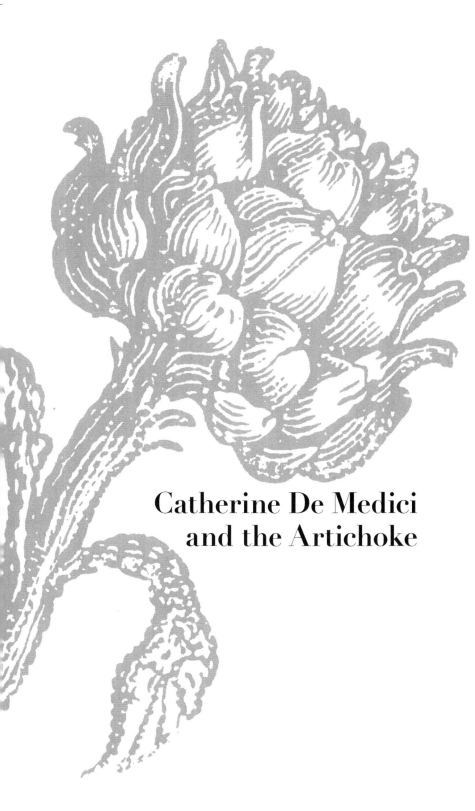

Catherine De Medici
and the Artichoke

Catherine de Medici and
the Artichoke

I can see her fingers plucking purple-green   petals from three
hundred and fifty years away,   see her drag her impertinent
teeth across their fine   flesh, discarding them as she swallows,
that buttery day
            in her fourteenth year she arrived to wed France,
calmly slit the bristled throat and stroke   the cervix-shaped
    artichoke bottom to rustles of *If once*   *any of us ladies had*
    eaten artichokes,

                we would have been pointed out on the street.
Catherine says, *I like to burst*. After   that several things happened. After
those, her sheathed body   (now her husband's deceased)
turns to the Queen mother—
             who from a bowl between her knees
is stuffing herself sick with artichoke bottoms,   and cockerel kidneys and
cockerel combs,

How to Use a Napkin

Understand the napkin
has been unnecessary
for most of human history.

Understand the world is filled with people
eager to bend
things to their will.
We shall practice on the napkin.
When you have finished eating
place your napkin loosely
next to your plate.

It should not be crumpled or twisted,
which would reveal untidiness or nervousness;
nor should it be folded,

which might be seen as an implication
that you think your hosts
might reuse it without washing.
.

It is a delicate affair.
Don't argue with me
said my husband

who had called for my advice
about the apartment he was renting
when he didn't want to live with me.

It is largely
symbolic today
except for barbecues.
Lightly dab the lips.

I suspect the word
argue is the space
in the mouth for things
to come apart in.

The napkin must not be left
on the chair, it might seem
as if you have an inappropriately

dirty napkin to hide
or even that you are trying
to run off with the table linens.

It takes great trust
to use a napkin.
It takes an act
of faith to leave
the table.

Finer Dining

Depleted claws of lobster clatter
onto wilted beds. Why
is it illicit lovers labor under
such predictable taste? The pinots,
noir and grigio, like brothers in a pert
Italian *tele novella*. Grigio
enjoys lake views, Robert Hass,
salads of sawed-off flowers.
Noir likes bloody steaks.
Can't you just imagine
moans between chopsticks
and a shower, saxophone horns
against the wall, one-trick ponies
kicking up their dusty little heels
in your bedroom. God
how you hate Banff
this time of year.

Oh your poppy seed,
oh your mint and dill,
shadows on the lawn, white linen,
this life you've so indelicately
and so deliberately liked.
Then the yellow citrus peel
curling along the lip
of a dessert espresso,
the existential meringue.
Yes, what lies between you
& forever isn't me.

Cooking with Emma Bovary

Eggs

Muffins were baked in their paper and tins, and then tins were overturned. Everyone was eating the day she turned out. What she turned out of no one could say, being so deeply implicated in the yard sale. But the chickens were a common denominator. The way their stubby wings began to yearn, wheeling to low-lying pine boughs for a stately finish. Or, in more disheveled air, skidding to a stop on the corrugated tin roof, shedding frantic commas, everything shimmering with unsteadiness.

Roosting is a prelude to roasting, or maybe turning in the duration. Morning was common. The chickens in stranger yards one by one had been replaced. Then the yards were selling their strangers off. Soon the strangers were only strange in the familiar way.

This is how population shifts, how landfloes through layers of languages, tongues always forking to the sea, or at least to the water table. Once in a while someone put the ice tray back in the freezer without filling it first. She always hated that.

Milk

The cows lived to be milked every day. It was necessary. To separate the calf from the cow took three people and some molasses. His sweet-smelling lashes, his dusty curls. But you grew bones and teeth, your grandfather was gored by an exclamation point. These contexts are now empty sockets that once held the molars. Or else they were the false teeth serene in the glass on the nightstand in that forbidden twilit room, those chilling lilac bath tiles. You have never been sure, since they ache with you and also in the without. Besides, those who live in glass slippers should spit the pebbles out and be quiet.

Flour

She could have gone through her entire life knowing nothing but low-born rustics, farmhands, villas and their villainy. But weren't the apprentices pretty preening over the twin mirrors of lake and sky, blowing the wheat from the chaff.

Cookbook

Coming from a shindig she fell into a comma. Its unscrupulous scoop slid down her derriere, cutting her off in mid
. The pebbles in her mouth were gleaming like breath. It was most cultivating. Soon the etch-a-sketch sky shook itself clear. There were shovels everywhere, and their little digged runes. How long she lay there. It was spelling, really.

Muffins

She left the house with all her machines whirring. Her laundry hangs to dry, like pages of letters for neighbors to read. In some lands the trains run faster than buses; in some the buses run faster than trains. Flats come with maids, with contingents of recycling bins, or with gas masks. There are no exceptions. Some countries don't distinguish between the cupcake and the muffin. The distinction is hard to articulate convincingly. But it's true that companion means the one who shares my bread.

Leshalem

To pay, to bring to a conclusion, bring to perfection,
to make peace.

i.

I am not a piece
of cake—sometimes
the eternal á
la mode, which is
to say, I am
your mouth, not your whole
mouth, just the part
that, when full, worries
about its next meal.

ii.

The eggs must first come
to room temperature,
which is to say for
everything there is
time. While the cotton
opened white fists at her
window, one by one
my grandmother beat
six eggs by hand till
they were stiff. The hands
of the kitchen clock
tapped each fat minute,
the ready spoon curved.
The frothy batter
she poured herself into
the tube pan steadied itself
in the wood-fueled oven
and lifted. Those who ate
a single bite were filled
with an inexplicable
happiness. Sometimes
that was enough.

Raspberry

Imagine a world:
your entire possession
a single raspberry

and you give it to
your friend. On Guerda's birthday
in Auschwitz, Ilse

found the raspberry
on the way to the fields,
swaddled it in a leaf,

slipped it in her pocket.
Then she plucked potatoes
all day from the artless

earth, all her movements
restricted by that
unexpected miracle.

It was, of course, an offense
punishable by death.
The fragrance that filled

the field, moved the air.
Its juice reddened as
the day bit its lip,

paced on, it became
the sun, became another
kind of calendar.

The Love Life of Objects

Josef Sudek, 1896–1976

i.

These are the objects light has groomed
in Josef Sudek's famously photographed studio:

a rain that wipes its fingerprints from the windowpane,
a tree that twists from earth to sky, unable to decide,

a plate of peaches freighted with the taste that never leaves
his mouth. Like other Czechs before him, he has confessed

to loving the secret life of objects.
Prague is full of them. One day he waits,

not under the net vaults of the spiny St. Vitus Cathedral,
hatching itself for six centuries through dust and hammer falls,

nor in the nave where the great stained glass windows
unfasten all morning their cobalt, fuchsia, green and gold

leaving them draped on the floors and scaffolding,
across the uneven shoulders of workmen balancing pails of paint,

but deep below street level in the Romanesque halls,
holding ready a single sleeve of dust.

There suddenly the light slips in, hungrily, fitfully filling it up.
He has waited all year for this day.

He fingers the shutter release
like the Italian soldier had fingered the trigger

of his own rifle twenty years before,
taking aim, as well, at a sunlit sleeve.

And—like a discarded lover
erases himself in a flash of pleasantries and pride

from the grouting of his beloved's mind,
—he presses the shutter release of his camera

vanishing over again and over again.

ii.

But when he leaves the cathedral, his own coat sleeve is still empty
as it's been since the war.

He remembers the day he returned to Italy
and stood over the sunny meadow where he lost his gangrened arm

muttering *you won't get away with it.*
And who was *you* and what was *it*

if not himself, his own secret negative.
And even Milena, his lover, complained

the more beautiful her image, the uglier she felt—so
he'd stir the dust before her

or place a screen between her and his eye, and carefully plumb
the imperfections of her face.

What one loves now, he knows, is nothing
compared to what was once so loved.

But soon what has always been there begins
to come in

to focus in the slow
skin it spreads out upon,

the freckled reflection
caught in a half-drunk coffee cup

though the girl who brought it is almost
gone.

Pomegranates

A snake
       is pouring himself up
a shattering of twigs.
              His shadow
strokes
       the dead gold leaves
                  on which the sun first practiced
          writing
       all its discarded names.
               Beneath his dappled skin
his muscles
              twitch
                 through currents of time
      so beautiful my brothers
           fidget
with the urge   to knock
                something down.
The stolen pomegranates
           that we pulled
from our   grandmother's   scrawny tree
     the seeds we broke   on the potholed
                  streets of town
         Like everything else
      forbidden
         they were hard and bitter   green.
     We've been spitting them out
              all our lives.

With little maps and legend

Happy are the sowers that will not reap
For they will wander a long way off.
Avraham Ben-Yitzhak

1. Where I was born spiders

made the 10-foot ruffs
we mistook for air. Problem
was, we wandered in.

To miracles, I mean.
Stronger than steel, springier
at the center, legs

luxuriously
banned, black and gold, rolling a
blurred wasp, a locust

before its shivers
tore the whole web down. So much
around here broken

it's almost of no
consequence. And hunger, the
emaciated

cat, swollen nipples,
kittens kneading her sides, a
pause, my mama

calling me back to
the dusting, which is really
just dirt pushed someplace

dynamic. So
fine it's almost gone.

2. In the family garden plot

ages of women
deeply skilled at digging up
potatoes, touching

what dumbly insists
on space, wash their hands in
water buckets, shake

off delicacies of air.

3. Repeatedly in Moravia

to the night-blind grave-
stones my old-world cousins bring
candlelight and wreathes

weaved with nervy hands
as is the custom. For a short time
earth pockets bodies:

until the poured lime
has licked the bones clean
for twenty years. Bones

courteously scooch
to make room for the next body.
Above the Roman

church, *Bud' vule tva'*
jako v nebi tak y na
zemi, on earth as in

heaven gets tangled
in trees, leaps over the roads
overwhelming cars'

And the hitchhiking
priest is out of breath and ten
minutes late for Mass.

(4. interlude of the Hapsburg monarchy

Dear Other Woman,
every morning now for weeks
I've felt your fingers
gently slide up through my throat
as I awoke.
I have felt your feet
kick my body from your sleep,
your toes clenched in my stomach,
your fingers, little knives.

Dear Other Woman, you
are neither here nor there.)

5. The cemetery and the overpass demonstrate the prairie

I'm reading the names of the dead
the photos on their stones tell us

they used to go to school and like to fish
and drink Coca-Cola one teenaged couple had a baby

whom they'd dropped at abuela's house before the hairpin
turn on the highway on his leave between tours in Afghanistan

these ones are new
they used to be buried in the Spanish cemetery

under the gnarled and stunted oaks
where cattle are now grazing behind their barbed wire fences

there is grass the sky bright blue
the chill wind remembers a pub

or a beer joint depending
warm beer and boots and smoke

there is not a tree in sight
the stones are carved in languages

I understand no need wonder who they're with
here they are now the camera lens

is scratched a bit the rubber grip is loosening
the hill was swelling then it stopped

a cloud blows across the sky
it all happened a long time ago

someone holding the pages of a letter
which pressed her skin like fingertips

you have removed one by one.

6. Once I lived something more romantic

by which I mean closer to long ago
            smell of the clay of the land
                        lap of waves, measure of breath
fishermen translate us with their lures
            and nets, everyone should slip at least
                        once behind phosphorescent flesh
of jellyfish (it needn't be so
            exotic as this, once it was flounder
                        fishing in the creek, anything
shimmering and past bedtime will do)
            dolphins galloping at the prow
                        rocks the sun touched earlier
still glowing Venezuela
            when the weather changes you find
                        yourself in Texas stewing pumpkins
boiling grapes till they part
            without a convincing narrative
                        melting honey to mix in flour
grinding cloves and ginger root
            brushing the fragrance on your jeans
                        moving in the mirrors of your windows
you hear pecans dropping on tin roofs
            wrists letting go of leaves
                        and because the ants are always busy
translating the natural world
            into the underworld, which is to say
                        the afterlife one grain, one blade,
one pigment a time, the leaves drop
            over ants in nests, in fallen
                        eye sockets, over bare feet
tiny pricks of conscience, twitches of fear
            a pillow bursts and feathers
                        reach for the memory of flight
a river shifts and the dry ones
            on the shore wave goodbye.

Dear Ahasuerus

Avera

crossing, violation

In Venezuela, we could whack the heads off these empty wine bottles, plant
their bottoms in fresh cement so their jagged teeth would flash between the
    rich
and those of the poor unemployed by the rich. If we were still
in Germany, there'd be a pragmatic plastic bin labeled *colored glass*, and there
they'd sleep it off, till someone hauled them to the rubber belt
they'd ride for free, be scrubbed and dried. They'd open
their mouths and be filled again. If we were still in Austin
or South Philly we'd be laughing so hard when they fell, we'd
gather their shards, and with mirrors (because the more
the merrier) and plastic glow-in-the-dark saints
we'd make the guys who piss against the walls at night
something nice to look at;

as Henry Ford said, art should be something for every day. Most workers on
large public projects in Mesopotamia got one liter of beer
a day. On the occasion of Queen Pu-abi's death (daily
allotment, six liters, with silver, gold and lapis straws, cased with marsh
    reeds)
twelve chamber maids, five male armed guards and two groomsmen were
    thrown
a banquet to die for. Literally. Had
I been there I would have looked longest at the rams rendered
in gold, silver and lapis lazuli—each raised on hind
legs, nibbling a shrub—coffee? At some point that
night, I would have dipped my cup into a copper
pot, like everyone else, and drunk it. The effect
was irreversible.

It's true my mother's angry children made me keep their vineyards while my own
I had not kept. But lately I've found myself possessed of stone jars full of
sweet and of breath that hovers just above the earth awhile. When
I taste it I don't know what is earth and what air, what is water, what fire, who
my mother's angry children are, where *never* ends where I
begin and what Pu-abi did with the key
to the death pit where the banquet was. The only thing worse
than being unloved is being loved above all others.
Ayin-bet-reysh pronounced *Avera*—means violation,
means moving, since at a certain point it's hard to
stop. Moving, from one word to the next because *ayin-bet-reysh*,
pronounced *Ivrit*, is language

or "Hebrew" and a state of existence if you happen to be Avram,
the first Hebrew, crossing a river from his and Queen Pu-abi's
hometown Ur into Canaan. Since then every age of wonder
has its own body of water, and the inconsolable who discover what
they crossed was sometimes only the usual kind of water,
which is why Baudelaire said *always be drunk*;
be drunk means be emptied or else filled, almost all the way,
but never at the same time. A tooth in the mouth of the
Gulf of Mexico, my grandfather reminds me
of Noah. First thing upon disembarking, his
native village obliterated, he planted
himself a vineyard, too.

The Casting of Lots

1.

Dear Ahasuerus, it is eleven-thirty am and my number is one hundred and eighty-six. I feel the lack of communion striving for a higher purpose in this government assistance office, and it is beyond sadness and feet and the distance of aircraft and tires and inner tubes on turgid rivers in midsummer with aluminum cans of beer. It's not just the ones who pick discarded numbers from the floor and say they missed their turn. The flower-selling prepubescent children sniffing glue in paper bags outside the margins of the magazine I'm reading remind me of the laundry I hung up that must be dry by now, filled as they are with warmth and wings and snapping.

When God withdraws, we all must breathe a little harder.

2.

Are these hosts the kind of people who refrigerate red wine? I wasn't breastfed, I smelled different. I never learned to desire consolation prizes. The water hisses from the tap, sliced by the tips of lettuce leaves. The cut-crystal conversation turns on the tiniest incisions. So little of it is about you, you have to address yourself as one of your second persons. At the click of one of our host's glances, each woman at the table presses forward, like a bullet into the chamber. It goes without saying, this is how I see myself among the women, Dear Ahasuerus, you fuck.

Union

Two small onions filled the eye-sockets of Ramses IV who lay stiff, as if awake
in the rusty crook of the Nile's arm (which, when viewed
from an aerial photo, resembles a scar
in the Valley of the Kings). Night falls swiftly there
and artists were assigned inspirations that endured longer than their lives,
precision carving tools, and strips
of cloth combed from the local weeds.

Onions in chest cavities, attached to the soles of the feet, in the pelvis, along
bald legs, molded in the ears, poised the expectant
body for its next breath in a bold pre-furnished
afterworld. They were red skinned, the same color as
Ramses IV's legendary hair. Their name
came when the onion-shaped letter *o*

slipped into *union*. A union is something invisible. Under investigation
it falls apart. But it's somewhat comforting to
me that even loss is never completely effaced.
After Pompei burned, the onion bulbs remained
as cavities beneath the scorched ground. Now draw me into your mouth and
    blow
me out, because I don't want to
be immortal, but thoroughly spent.

Desire

The wind was awhirl with petals until I didn't know what it was
        I had conceived, the leaky tidal basin,
awash with white petals, the round of sky awash

and I between in a wrap-around cotton dress, a season's frill,
        the air staggering into my lungs, *our imperfections*, the pool
a clapper the petals pealed

accustoming us to desire, the mirrored sky, like the copper mirrors
        the Israelite women carried in Egypt?—I should
say now, this pregnancy wasn't planned—who went to draw water,

and God would adorn their buckets
        with little fish which they would sell
for wine. They made themselves up,

then brought their men the fish they'd saved and cooked,
        and wine. They would wrap
their arms around them, and lift the mirror, accustoming

them to desire. How my mother
        made my sister
spit into the Kleenex then wipe the blue

eye shadow in the Dodge Ram van on the way to town. For years
        it seemed *she seduced me* meant *she didn't say no*.
Though how many of the work-sore men asked themselves, "What

have I done?" once the jug, emptied of its wine, lay snoring
        on its side, the fish bones combing
the scraggly grass, the fire smoking, mirrors asleep in the hands

of the naked wives. Our vocabulary
>for describing the virtues of women remains surprisingly
limited. *Dear Parents: On Thursday we will be having a little*

Passover Seder in the Gan. If you can please send your child
>*with a hard-boiled egg*
and some lettuce that would be wonderful. I am becoming

accustomed to certain kinds of desire.
>Tonight, on my Tel Aviv balcony, I am watching the fruit
bats devour red bulbs

of the cotton tree. I am watching their tongues and teeth.
>It isn't easy.
For one thing, I stutter,

desire full of mercy, and mercy a kind of desire.

Hebrew Lesson: Lichbosh

To conquer, occupy, preserve

Before bowls and jugs existed
there were clay walls around
Jericho—its name
means fragment, and sometimes,
it means moon. How to enter it
is crucial. Wise to have spies when you're circling perfection
that isn't your own: The woman, the innkeeper Rehab,
plunged her nail to its half-moon
into the belly of a fig. She looked up and said, *Remember me and my family,*
as if she were tethered
by scarlet threads to a longing that well-furnished orchards can't fill.

At the border of the Promised
Land, men occupy all
the front row seats each night,
weeping silently. *You*
have ravished my heart, my sister,
my bride you have ravished with one glance of your eyes, with one
jewel of your necklace, they say, meaning *you can go now.*
What would you have them do?
Everyone hungers, especially for hunger. Jericho: belly of an old bowl,
drain of ancient sinks, the
air shimmering with sheaves of wheat, barley, peas pinging into plates,

and palms. Two thousand years later,
in the city of psalms,
a woman said *I'm*
tired as David picked her
up. They had drinks. He took her home.
She got undressed, walked into his bedroom and lay down. She

just lay there, as if she were asleep. You can't just lie there
waiting to get serviced
with David, as if you were Denmark after Germany invaded. The problem
with beautiful girls is
that they always end up peasants on the land they once possessed.

Tamar, who studied dancing on
the knuckles of desire,
finally got her own.
Though her face covered
like a whore. How readily Judah
had given up staff and seal. *Oh little boys inside your
mother's lovely womb, your mother's a sentence she can't stand
to have completed. Your
mother is one line of an unrhymed couplet, three unrhymed. Did you think you
        could just break,
enter and leave without
a trace, Judah? No one can.* Now the Israeli intelligence

seduction program is trying
to recruit female spies
with its pragmatic
name, *honeytrap*. Rabbis
across the land sanction them to
abandon children and chicken soup, to sleep in virile
arms of strangers, and here's the thing. Like Tamar, all David's
second wife wanted in
the end, after the parties, the unbelievable toys, was a baby. Isn't that
all any of us want,
to possess what someone else desires, be what someone else

desires? Those breasts like figs
ripening under
an emphatic tongue.
It is an old story:

How Xerxes, the defeated King,
ordered that figs from Attica be served him at every
meal to remind him that he no longer possessed the land
on which they grew.

Language Exchange: Anguish

In every western language, anger
is conceived in anguish, a special kind of pain,
akin to strangulation or throttling:

angus, enge, enghe, aggwus
amhu, ankhein, angere. Even Latin and Greek
agree, narrowness, want, torment.

Sometimes when I am alone
I take off my wedding rings.
Simon Weil says our egos rise

to fill the space they're given.
Nature despises a vacuum.
And I despise a vacuum cleaner.

Anger is conceived in confinement.
Its aspiration in life is to die
swaddled in scarves of emptiness, blessed space.

On the shore of the Mediterranean,
every grain of sand predetermined as ancestors,
watch the measured distance

where ships laden with arms, oil, spices,
fish and sweet drinking water push
across the blueprints of our horizon.

I place my rings among the tomatoes and onions
in the ceramic bowl made by silent nuns
of Beit Jamal. The onion had to break something

luminous and perfect
to come into being. Now it radiates
blank on blank on blank.

Holy

If to be holy
means to be set apart,
then keep the wound open until it no longer

resembles a wound,
but a constant tenderness.
In marriage it applies to women, what men make

of them. The difference
between a kept woman
and a wife is contractual. Every woman wants

to be her own
agent. But, holy, you
must lose an integral part. For the sole purpose

of not gaining
anything in return.
This is called grace—a permeable emptiness.

(Keep it open.
Keep it embryonic.)
It is the boudoir of the ego. This is a kind

of prayer. Or
even prayer's definition.

Jerusalem

In the covered shuk an orange was the only source of light,
the spices snored in canvass bags all night in Jerusalem.

There are always scored stones above, curtains, flags below,
shifting their gravity from shoe to shoe in tight-fitting Jerusalem.

The cracks in the Western Wall are soaked in prayers,
the doves are scraps of light above Jerusalem.

The Mount of Olives crouches over the Wailing Wall:
bleached bone, bleached stone, sun-crumbled white Jerusalem.

Like teeth broken on what they've been given to say,
rows and rows of white boxes, asleep against the might of Jerusalem.

Bullet holes are horizontal, rain-bored holes are vertical.
The pools, the ritual baths fill themselves in the sight of Jerusalem.

No other city has drunk so much ink;
who from the sages would know how to write, but for Jerusalem?

Marriage
Flesh of My Flesh, Bone of My Bone

A bone stretched to its full length, in its private
burial cave, or a bone oblivious of light,

of lust and of teeth? A bone over which
bitches have fought. It's picked clean on a polished

floor. A bone turning over its dreaming
soil? A bone clicking under floorboards, knocking

on closet doors. A bone tied senseless
to other bones. When she pulls certain strings

it will raise him. And when they grow old
they will line up the bones, matching black dots,

like saturated eyes that give nothing away?
They will roll the bones, just when they

feel most secure. Later Venetian Carnivals will conceive
dominoes, and the winter habits of French priests

(white outside, black within) will bestow the moniker.
But Queen Jezebel would have never

pronounced the word *dominus*, except in jest.
And dice (singular, die) can come to rest

in six different attitudes, like a woman,
it means something played, something given.

Jezebel: most maligned applier of eyeliner?
Most hated defier of fate, deifiers

of history have ever known. She was to me
a sulky husband's spine, last seen

working her fingers to the bone. Delicate
anklebones, kohl-blackened eyes in a white face?

He keeps calling her—his little deuce—through the grow-
ing pains of all the comely adolescent bones.

Brinksmanship

Six speakers in a ten-meter room in downstairs Tel Aviv, all the doors and windows open, turning the boulevard into my neighbor's private dance floor. There he is with a coy little step, tossing his head and fluttering his fingertips over his shoulder. The crowd on his balcony laughing and clapping. Even I can see it's adorable.

The plates on their drying rack in my kitchen, one floor above, are clapping as well, the vibrations nudging them off the shelf.

My daughter asks, "What are you going to fix?" as my hammer guides me down the stairs. Because there isn't enough happiness in the world, because there is not enough space. And someone's pleasure will always come at the expense of another. Because they had chosen me to pay, calling me *bitch* behind my back. There are not enough resources in the world. And those who have no inner resources are the worst jerks of all. But I don't want to pay today. Because today there is nothing worse than trying to live with God's chosen people in the land that God gave to them. Because *if you are scared to go to the brink, you are lost.*

They said, "Hey lady, no need for violence." They said, "What kind of mother are you, to let a child see you with a weapon like this." But the party was over in a heartbeat. Garbage gathered, revelers swept into the street. I turned, my child stood trusting me, wide-eyed in the stairwell.

Mercy, a double sonnet

In Jerusalem everyone eats mercy, is reeking
with it. The kohled and veiled woman on the #19 bus traces
her desire onto paper slipped between her filigree ring
and her finger, then on her cell phone album the six faces

of her children appear one by one like the fresh light of stars
that has taken so long to arrive here. How "similar"
sometimes means "near." Pinches-on-the-cheek and kisses for ours.
Everyone has something to give: the falafel stand owner

has free chips for children, the next-door florist, his revolutionary
method of watering geraniums, his appreciation
for the pockets on Amalia's dress, his mastery
of American show tunes, his convenient location.

A girl descends from the #32, the stretch marks rise
from her low-rise skinny jeans between her
dark-skinned narrow hips—her black hair piled high,
the impossible stacked heels. Let her

be who she is. Let everyone have correct change, let everyone
change somehow to make room
for the plump menopausal Hungarian
on the #405 to Bnei Berak, with her two

private bags and her beads of sweat. I was so ungracious
it was a relief, the swiftness of her justice: *I am soorrrry.*
I vas rrrong she notes, *That **VAS** your stop vee pass.*
Her tongue flopping like unbound breasts—look at me,

I'm doing it again—under a quilted housedress. Atone:
Coins for the whiney, coins for the cheeky, coins
for the intimate urging voice,
from the folds of your complicated wallet, the rolls of your fat, juicy purse.

Notes

La Malinche's Love Letters to Fernando Cortés
La Malinche was a Nahau (Aztec) woman. According to Cortés's
biographer, Bernal Diaz del Castillo (see *Historia Verdadera de la Conquista
de la Nueva Espana*) she was born of a noble family on the border region
between the Mayan and the Aztec empires. When her father died, her
mother remarried and bore a son, and she was sold to slave traders. She
eventually came into the possession of Cortés, the Conquistador who led
the expedition that caused the downfall of the Aztec empire.
Section 5: italicized portion comes from *Dark Night of the Soul* by John of the
Cross.
Section 6: italicized portion is a rephrasing of Witold Gombrowicz's *Diary
Volume 3*. p. 88.

Avera. The Hebrew alphabet consists only of consonants, written from
right to left. Almost all Hebrew words are composed of a three-letter root.
Vowels are indicated by diacritical marks. So that the words for Hebrew,
violation, crossing, and moving all come from the same 3-letter root, רבע.

The Casting of Lots refers to the story of Purim, found in the book of
Esther. Ahasuerus, the King of Persia, is also called Xerxes. The Book of
Esther, in which this story is recounted, is the only book of the Hebrew
Bible that does not contain the word "God."

Lichbosh refers to Biblical story of Moses' predecessor, Joshua, sending
spies into the land of Canaan before he attempted to occupy it. Rehab is an
innkeeper who lived in the city walls of Jericho and protected the spies in
exchange for their protection when they returned to conquer the city.
See *Joshua* 2.

The City of Psalms refers to Jerusalem. The City of David, built by King
David, to whom the Biblical psalms are attributed, is located just outside
Jerusalem's Old City walls.

Tamar was the daughter-in-law of Judah, one of the twelve sons of Jacob (Israel). She married Judah's first two sons, one after the other, and each died childless. When Judah withheld his third son, who was obligated, by law, to give Tamar a child in is brother's name, Tamar veiled herself like a prostitute and became pregnant with Judah's child. See Genesis 38.

Xerxes is also called Ahasuerus in Hebrew, and is the king Esther marries in the Jewish story of Purim.

Acknowledgments

The author is grateful to the editors of the following journals and anthologies for previously publishing poems from this collection, sometimes in slightly different forms:

The Bakery: "Leshalem" and "The Casting of Lots"

Black Warrior Review: "Lichbosh"

Canteen: "Catherine De Medici and the Artichoke" and "The History of the Papaya"

The Cimarron Review: "Union"

Cortland Review: "Jerusalem"

Fence: "Avera"

Forklift Ohio. A journal of light industry and public safety: "How to Use a Napkin"

Guernica : "Marriage, Flesh of my Flesh, Bone of my Bone"

The Journal: "Cooking with Emma Bovary"

The Minnesota Review: "Ecclesiastes"

New Letters: "Chocolate" and "Finer Dining"

No Tell Motel: "A Body in Labor"

Poet Lore: "The Love Life of Objects"

Rattle: "Men on Strike"

Recours au poème: "Raspberry" and "With little maps and legend," bilingual. French trans. Sabine Huynh

Salamander: "Decency"

Southeast Review: "Pomegranates"

Spoon River Review: "La Malinche's LoveLetters to Fernando Cortés" and "Mercy, a double sonnet"

Tikkun Magazine: "Translation depends, not on what must be included, but on what must not be left out"

Tupelo Quarterly: "Louise, TX"

Yew Journal: "Holy," originally published as "Hebrew Lesson: Kidesh," "Language Exchange: Anguish," and "Brinksmanship"

"The Love Life of Objects" is reprinted in *From a Terrace in Prague. A Prague Poetry Anthology.*

"Ecclesiastes" and "Jerusalem" are reprinted in *The Bloomsbury Anthology of Contemporary Jewish American Poetry.*

"Holy" is reprinted as "Hebrew Lesson: Kidesh" in the essay "Getting a Get," runner up in the 2012 *Iowa Review* Nonfiction Competition.

"Louise, TX" is reprinted in English and translated into French by Sabine Huynh in *Recours au poème.*

"Men on Strike" was reprinted in Verse Daily.

Thank you, Steve Gehrke, Brandel France de Bravo, Carol Quinn, Nancy Carlson, Joelle Biele, Andrea Baker, Idra Novey, Molly Sutton Kiefer, for feedback on the manuscript and poems. Thank you, Isela Verduga and Marva Zohar, and thank you, the poet mothers. Thank you for the space in which to work, and the friendship with which it was shared, Caitlin McDonald, Roz Singer & Robby Bindiger, Scotti Sulak, Abe Louise Young, Sarah Van Arsdale & Peter Bricklebank, Tomáš Míka & Letizia Kostner, Marka Míkova, Jane & Jon Medved and Joanna & Raz Chen. Thank you, Diane Goettel!

Photo: Daniel Fainberg

Marcela Sulak's previous poetry collections include *Immigrant* (BLP, 2010) and the chapbook *Of all the things that don't exist, I love you best*. She's translated four collections of poetry from Israel, the Czech Republic, and the Democratic Republic of the Congo. Her nonfiction has appeared in *The Iowa Review, The Los Angeles Review of Books* and *Rattle*. She's an editor at *The Tupelo Review* and *The Ilanot Review,* and she directs the Shaindy Rudoff Graduate Program in Creative Writing at Bar-Ilan University, where she teaches poetry and American literature. She lives in Tel Aviv.